Pizza
COOKBOOK

**Delicious and Zesty Dishes
That Make Life More Flavorful.**

Mud Puddle Books
NEW YORK

Pizza Cookbook

© 2006
R&R Publications Marketing Pty. Ltd.

This edition published by
Mud Puddle Books, Inc.
54 W. 21st Street
Suite 601
New York, NY 10010
info@mudpuddlebooks.com

ISBN: 1-59412-117-6

Originally published by
R&R Publications Marketing Pty. Ltd.
12 Edward Street, Brunswick
Victoria 3056 Australia

Printed and bound in China

contents

contents

introduction

Pizza can trace its origins as far back as ancient Egypt, Greece and Rome.

By the end of the 18th century, pizza was one of the favorite dishes of the people—and royalty—of Naples. Neapolitan pizzerias came into existence during these years, the most famous of which, 'Pietro ... e basta Così', was opened by Pietro Colicchio in 1780. Because Colicchio had no sons, the pizzeria was left to his partner Enrico Brandi. Eventually the name was changed to the Pizzeria Brandi. The pizzeria maintains that name to this day while continuing the traditions established by Colicchio more than 225 years ago.

In 1889, the King of Naples Ferdinando di Borbone was entertaining Umberto I and his wife Queen Margherita, members of the royal house of Savoia and the reigning King and Queen of Italy. Di Borbone invited Raffaele Esposito, Enrico Brandi's son-in-law and the greatest pizza maker of his day, to make pizzas for the royal family. Queen Margherita particularly liked the pizza made with pomodoro (tomato) and mozzarella. This pizza was named 'Pizza Margherita' and that is the name by which it is still known today.

The love of pizza spread from Naples to the rest of Italy and then to the rest of the world. Today pizzas range from standard take-out fare to gourmet wood-fired delights.

You can cook pizzas in your own home using the range of exciting recipes in this cookbook. Once you've mastered the pizza-making technique, use the following recipe for basic pizza dough and create your own original pizza creations!

Basic pizza dough

1 tsp active dry yeast

pinch of sugar

2 cups plain flour

$^{1}/_{2}$ tsp salt

$^{1}/_{4}$ cup olive oil

1 Place the yeast, sugar and water in a large bowl and mix to dissolve. Set aside in a warm, draft-free place for 5 minutes or until foamy.

2 Place the flour and salt in a food processor and pulse once or twice to sift. With machine running, slowly pour in the oil and yeast mixture and process to form a rough dough. Turn the dough onto a lightly floured surface and knead for 5 minutes or until soft and shiny. Add more flour if necessary.

3 Lightly oil a large bowl, then roll the dough around in the bowl to cover the surface with oil. Cover the bowl tightly with plastic food wrap and place in a warm, draft-free place for $1^{1}/_{2}$ –2 hours or until the dough has doubled in volume. Knock down and remove from the bowl. Knead briefly before using as desired.

Makes *10 oz (300 g) dough*

Variations of pizza dough

Herb pizza dough: Add 1 teaspoon dried mixed herbs to the flour mixture.

Cheese pizza dough: Add 2 oz (60 g) of a grated tasty cheese (such as a mature Cheddar) to the flour mixture.

Tomato pizza dough: Replace the water with ²/₃ cup tomato juice – you will need to warm the tomato juice.

Whole-wheat pizza dough: Replace half the flour with whole-wheat flour. You may need to add a little extra water.

pizza
snacks

pizza boats

Dough

6½ oz (185 g) plain flour

6½ oz (185 g) self-rising flour

1 tbsp olive oil

2 eggs

½ tsp salt

5 tbsp warm water

Filling

1 medium-sized eggplant

1 cup olive oil

1 large onion, peeled and diced

1 large red pepper, seeded and chopped

2 cloves garlic finely chopped

2 cups basic tomato sauce (see page 17)

1 tbsp chopped herbs (oregano, parsley, basil)

¼ tsp ground coriander

salt and pepper

4 slices of salami

freshly grated Parmesan cheese (optional).

1 Sift the flours into a large mixing bowl and make a well in the center. Place the oil, eggs and salt in the well and gradually combine with the flour until all the dough ingredients are well mixed. (Your hands are the best kitchen implement for this process.) Add the water, a tablespoon at a time, to make a firm, smooth paste. Knead well for several minutes, then rest the dough, covered with a cloth, before rolling. (A hand-cranked rolling and cutting pasta machine is ideal if you have one.) Roll the dough evenly into thin sheets approximately ⅛ in (3 mm) thick, then cut into small oval boat shapes 2 in (5 cm) long. Line the boat-shaped molds with the dough shapes.

Serves *4*   ***Preparation*** *20 mins*   ***Cooking*** *40–50 mins*
Calories *1183*   ***Fat*** *75g*

2 Meanwhile, prepare the filling by slicing the eggplant in half lengthwise, then into strips 1 in (2 cm) thick. Cut the strips in half across the middle. Heat the olive oil in a pan and cook the eggplant until soft and just turning brown. Remove from the oil and drain on kitchen paper. Fry the onion and pepper in the pan and cook until soft. Return the eggplant to the pan with the onion mixture. Add the garlic, basic tomato sauce, herbs, ground coriander, salt and pepper. Stir gently to avoid breaking the eggplant, and cook the mixture for another 15 minutes on medium heat.

3 When the ratatouille mixture cools, fill the pizza dough boats, making sure a large piece of dark eggplant skin faces up on each. Decorate the tops with thin strips of salami or sprinkle with a little grated Parmesan cheese. Place in a preheated oven at 380°F and cook for 15–20 minutes.

4 small pita breads or 1
large pita bread

4 tsp butter, softened

about 1 cup tomato
sugo (natural tomato
pulp) or your favorite
tomato pasta sauce

olive oil

$1/2$ cup grated Parmesan
cheese

pizza
snacks

Topping 1

1 slice cooked ham,
bologna, or sausage,
cut into strips

1 small tomato, sliced

1–2 slices Swiss cheese
or Cheddar

6 stuffed olives, halved

Topping 2

4 slices salami

2 anchovies, halved

$1/2$ red pepper, sliced

2 tbsp grated Gruyère,
Swiss or Cheddar cheese

Topping 3

1 slice pineapple, cut up

8 slices pepperoni or
other salami

4 black olives

$1/2$ cup grated Swiss or
Cheddar cheese

Topping 4

6–8 mushrooms, sliced

$1/2$ red or green cap-
sicum, sliced

1–2 slices Swiss or
Cheddar cheese

1 Smear butter over the breads and toast under a
preheated grill. Heat the tomato sugo or sauce and
spread generously over each pita or, if using a large
pita, use different toppings for each quarter, ending
with cheese. Sprinkle olive oil and Parmesan over each
pizza and bake in a preheated oven at 400°F for
10–15 minutes or until golden and crisp around the
edges. Alternatively, grill under a preheated grill,
ensuring there is space between the pizzas.

Serves 4 **Preparation** 10 mins **Cooking** 20 mins **Calories** 672 **Fat** 44g

pita pizzas

4 small or 1 large
pita bread

1 cup tomato sugo
(natural tomato pulp) or
your favorite tomato
pasta sauce

4 slices pastrami or
smoked beef or 6 slices
beef salami, cut into
strips

1 red or green pepper,
cut into strips

2 tbsp shredded Gruyère
or Cheddar cheese

¹/₂ cup grated Parmesan
cheese (optional)

Serves *4* **Preparation** *10 mins*
Cooking *15 mins* **Calories** *226* **Fat** *9g*

1 Toast the pita bread under a preheated grill. Heat
the tomato sugo or sauce and spread over each pita.
Scatter the meat and pepper over the pita and top
with cheese. Bake the pizzas in a preheated oven at
400°F for 10–15 minutes or until golden and crisp
around the edges. Alternatively, place under a preheated grill, positioning not too close to the grill to
prevent burning. Cut the large pizza into four.

spinach
and goat's cheese pita pizza

4 oz (125 g) sun-dried tomatoes in oil, drained, plus 2 tbsp oil from the jar

2 tbsp tomato paste

1 clove garlic, roughly chopped

2 tsp finely chopped fresh thyme or ½ tsp dried thyme

8 oz (250 g) baby spinach

6 mini pita breads

6 cherry tomatoes, quartered

3 oz (100 g) soft goat's cheese, sliced

1 tbsp sesame seeds

1 Preheat the oven to 450°F. Blend the sun-dried tomatoes, tomato paste and garlic to a purée in a food processor or by using a hand blender. Mix in the thyme.

2 Bring a pan of water to the boil, immerse the spinach then remove and refresh in a bowl of cold water. Drain, then drizzle the sun-dried tomato oil over the top.

3 Spread the tomato and garlic purée over the pita breads and top with the spinach. Scatter the cherry tomatoes over, along with the cheese and sesame seeds. Cook for 10 minutes or until the cheese has melted slightly and started to brown.

Serves 6   **Preparation** 15 mins   **Cooking** 10 mins   **Calories** 153   **Fat** 5g

vegetarian
pizza

vegetable pizza

1 ready-made pizza base or prepared dough (see page 5), about 10 in (25 cm) in diameter

5 large button mushrooms, sliced

1 onion, cut into thin wedges

1 large zucchini, cut into thin diagonal slices

3 yellow squash, thinly sliced

2 tbsp olive oil

4–5 tbsp tomato paste

4–6 sun-dried tomatoes, cut into strips

lemon juice

pepper

1 Place the pizza base on an oiled baking sheet. Place in a preheated oven at 450°F and bake for 10 minutes to ensure a crisp base (do not turn the oven off).

2 Brush the mushrooms, onion, zucchini and squash with olive oil and grill, turning frequently, until just tender but not brown.

3 Brush the pizza base with extra oil, spread with the tomato paste to within 1 in (2½ cm) of the rim and arrange the vegetables on top. Return to the oven and bake for a further 8–10 minutes. Remove from the oven and scatter the tomato strips over. Squeeze over some lemon juice and season with pepper.

Serves 4   **Preparation** 25 mins   **Cooking** 20 mins
Calories 522   **Fat** 24g

Base

1 1/2 tsp dry yeast

1 cup warm water

1 tsp sugar

3 cups plain flour

3 tbsp olive oil

1 tsp salt

Topping

1 tbsp olive oil

10 oz (300 g) jar salsa dip of choice

1 onion, sliced

mushrooms, sliced

a little more olive oil to drizzle over pizza

tasty cheese, grated

salt and pepper, to taste

sprinkle oregano leaves

Serves 4–6
Preparation 10 mins
Cooking 20–25 mins
Calories 520
Fat 7g

famous
mushroom pizza

1 Dissolve the yeast in the warm water with the sugar. Let stand until it foams. Sift the flour into a bowl and add the yeast mixture, olive oil and salt. Mix to combine and set aside until doubled in size.

2 Turn out onto a floured board and knead to form a soft dough.

3 Press a piece of the dough, about the size of a tennis ball, onto a pizza tray. (You could use a cone tray or even a large baking dish.)

4 Brush the pizza base with the olive oil, spread liberally with salsa, then add the onion and mushrooms. Drizzle with more olive oil and cover liberally with the cheese, salt and pepper. Sprinkle with the oregano leaves.

5 Place in a preheated oven at 430°F for 20–25 minutes.

Italian pizza

Serves *4*   **Preparation** *20 mins*   **Cooking** *20–25 mins*
Calories *474*   **Fat** *2g*

1.1lb (500 g) plain flour

1 cup water

½ oz (15 g) yeast

2 oz (60 mL) carrot juice
(adds a golden color to
crust; you may substitute
water if desired)

½ tsp salt

Tomato sauce

3 tomatoes, diced

juice of 2 tomatoes

2 basil leaves, chopped

1 clove garlic

pinch of oregano

1   Make a well in the flour. Mix 2 oz (50 mL) of
water with the yeast and pour into the well in the
flour along with the carrot juice, remaining water
and salt. Mix together to form a dough. Knead the
dough and place in warm area to rest and rise.

2   For the sauce, cook the tomatoes, tomato juice, basil, garlic and oregano, sim-
mering until the sauce has reduced. Spread the sauce onto the pizza dough.

3   Add your favorite toppings. Examples include mushrooms, salami, olives,
mozzarella cheese.

4   Bake at 430°F for 20–25 minutes, or until cooked.

supreme

pizza

1 large red pepper	2 tbsp tomato paste
1 eggplant, cut in half	4 oz (125 g) salami, cut into strips
1/2 cup cup water	
2 cups self-rising flour	1 large tomato, sliced or cut into wedges
1 clove garlic, crushed	
1 tsp dried basil or oregano	14 oz (400 g) canned artichoke hearts, drained and cut into quarters
1/2 cup milk	
1 tbsp olive oil	3 1/2 cups mozzarella cheese, grated

1 Place the pepper in a shallow dish with the eggplant and water. Cover, place in a preheated oven at 400°F and bake for 20 minutes or until soft. (Do not turn the oven off.) Remove the covering and set aside to cool.

2 Sift the flour into a bowl and add the garlic, oregano, milk and oil. Mix to a soft dough. Place the dough on a floured surface and knead until smooth. Roll out into a circle large enough to cover an oiled 11 in (28 cm) pizza tin.

3 Remove the seeds and skin from the pepper and cut into thick slices. Scoop out the eggplant pulp using a spoon, and place in a bowl. Combine with the tomato paste and spread over the pizza base. Arrange the remaining ingredients on top, finishing with the cheese. Place the pizza in the oven and bake for 20–25 minutes or until the crust is golden brown and the cheese has melted.

mozzarella

cauliflower
cheese and mushroom pizza

1.1lb (500 g) cauliflower, cut into small florets

1 tbsp vegetable oil

1 red onion, sliced

4½ oz (125 g) mushrooms, sliced

1 packaged 12 in (30 cm) deep and crispy pizza base, or 1 quantity pizza dough (see page 5)

5 tbsp pizza topping or tomato purée (sieved tomatoes)

4½ oz (125 g) Red Leicester cheese, grated (substitute Cheddar, if desired)

12 oz (350 g) carton fresh cheese sauce

black pepper

2 tbsp snipped fresh chives

Serves 4 **Preparation** 20 mins
Cooking 25 mins **Calories** 737 **Fat** 43g

1 Preheat the oven to 430°F. Place the cauliflower florets in a saucepan, cover with boiling water and bring back to the boil. Cover and simmer for 5 minutes or until just tender, then drain well and return to the pan.

2 Meanwhile, heat the oil in a large frying pan and fry the onion for 2 minutes, stirring. Add the mushrooms and fry for another 2 minutes, stirring, until slightly softened, then set aside. Place the pizza base on a baking tray, spread with the pizza topping or tomato purée and sprinkle over half the Red Leicester (or Cheddar).

3 Stir the cheese sauce into the cauliflower florets and season. Spoon the mixture onto the pizza, top with the onion and mushroom mixture, then sprinkle with the remaining Red Leicester (or Cheddar) and chives. Bake for 15 minutes or until the cheese has just started to melt and turn golden brown.

easy
chili bean pizza

Serves 4 **Preparation** 7 mins **Cooking** 15–20 mins
Calories 785 **Fat** 37g

10 in (25 cm) pizza base
or 1 quantity pizza
dough (see page 5)

14 oz (400 g) canned
Mexican chili beans

2 jalapeño chilies, seed-
ed and sliced

8 oz (250 g) grated
mozzarella cheese

freshly ground black
pepper, to taste

1 oz (30 g) packet corn
chips

3 tbsp sour cream

1 Place the pizza base on a lightly greased baking tray and top with the beans. Sprinkle with the chilies, mozzarella cheese and black pepper.

2 Bake for 15–20 minutes or until the base is crisp and golden. To serve, top the pizza with the corn chips and sour cream.

goat's cheese and

Polenta base

3½ oz (100 g) self-rising flour

5½ oz (155 g) polenta

2 eggs, lightly beaten

¾ cup milk

1 tbsp olive oil

Red pepper topping

3 tbsp tomato paste

2 red peppers, roasted
and skins removed

5½ oz (125 g) button
mushrooms, sliced

5½ oz (125 g) marinated
eggplant

5½ oz (125 g) goat's cheese,
crumbled or chopped

1 tbsp fresh oregano or ½ tsp
dried oregano

freshly ground black pepper,
to taste

1 To make the base, place the flour and polenta in a bowl. Make a well in the center and stir in the eggs and milk to form a smooth batter.

2 Heat the oil in a 10 in (25 cm) heavy-based frying pan over a medium heat. Pour in the batter and cook for 5 minutes. Carefully turn the base over in the pan and cook for 5 minutes longer. Remove pan from the heat.

3 For the topping, spread the base with tomato paste and top with red pepper, mushrooms, eggplant, goat's cheese, oregano and black pepper to taste.

4 Place the pizza in a pan under a preheated hot grill and cook for 3 minutes or until the topping is hot. Serve hot or cold, cut into wedges.

polenta pizza

puff mushroom pizza

13 oz (375 g) prepared
puff pastry

2 oz (60 g) grated
Parmesan cheese

4½ oz (125 g) grated
mozzarella cheese

1 onion, thinly sliced

7 oz (200 g) mush-
rooms, sliced

3 tomatoes, cut into
⅜ in (1 cm) slices

10 pitted black olives

2 tsp chopped fresh
oregano or ½ tsp dried
oregano

2 tsp chopped fresh
thyme or ½ tsp dried
thyme

1 Roll out the pastry to fit a flat greased 10 in x
12½ in (26 x 32 cm) baking pan.

2 Sprinkle the pastry with Parmesan cheese and mozzarella cheese, then top with onion, mushrooms,
tomatoes and olives. Sprinkle with oregano and thyme
and bake at 400°F for 30 minutes or until the pastry is
puffed and golden. Serve hot, warm or cold.

*Note: This quick pastry-based pizza is great for weekend
meals and leftovers are ideal for packed lunches.*

Serves *6*   **Preparation** *12 mins*   **Cooking** *30 mins*
Calories *370*   **Fat** *22g*

red

onion, zucchini and tomato pizza

1 tbsp olive oil, plus extra for greasing

2 small red onions, sliced

1 yellow pepper, deseeded and sliced

2 small zucchinis, sliced

1 clove garlic, crushed

9 oz (250 g) plain whole-wheat flour

2 tsp baking powder

2 oz (55 g) margarine

3⅓ oz (100 mL) reduced-fat milk

4 tbsp tomato purée

1 tbsp tomato paste

2 tsp dried mixed herbs

black pepper

3 small plum tomatoes, sliced

3⅓ oz (100 g) reduced-fat mature Cheddar, grated

fresh basil to garnish (optional)

Serves 4   **Preparation** 20 mins
Cooking 30–35 mins   **Calories** 466   **Fat** 24g

1 Preheat the oven to 430°F. Heat the oil in a saucepan, then add the onions, pepper, zucchinis and garlic and cook for 5 minutes or until softened, stirring occasionally. Set aside.

2 Place the flour and baking powder in a bowl, then rub in the margarine. Stir in the milk to form a smooth dough and knead lightly.

3 Roll out the dough on a lightly floured surface to a circle about 10 in (25 cm) wide and place on a greased baking sheet. Mix together the tomato purée, tomato paste, mixed herbs and black pepper and spread over the dough. Top with the onion mixture.

4 Arrange the tomato slices on top and sprinkle with Cheddar. Bake for 25–30 minutes, until the cheese is golden brown and bubbling. Garnish with fresh basil.

barbecue
pumpkin

Basic pizza dough

I tsp active dry yeast

pinch sugar

$^2/_3$ cup warm water

2 cups plain flour

$^1/_2$ tsp salt

$^1/_4$ cup olive oil

Pumpkin feta topping

I tbsp olive oil

8 large slices pumpkin, peeled and seeds removed

I onion, sliced

$10^1/_2$ oz (300 g) feta cheese, crumbled

I tbsp chopped fresh thyme

freshly ground black pepper, to taste

I Place the yeast, sugar and water in a bowl and mix to dissolve. Set aside in a warm, draught-free place for 5 minutes or until the mixture is foamy.

2 Place the flour and salt in a food processor and pulse once or twice to sift. With the machine running, slowly pour in the yeast mixture and oil and process to form a rough dough. Turn the dough onto a lightly floured surface and knead for 5 minutes or until soft and shiny. Add more flour if necessary.

3 Place the dough in a lightly oiled large bowl; roll the dough around the bowl to cover the surface with oil. Cover the bowl with plastic food wrap and place in a warm draught-free place for $1-1^1/_2$ hours or until doubled in size. Knock down and knead lightly.

4 Preheat the barbecue to a high heat. To make the topping, heat the oil on the barbecue plate for 2–3 minutes or until hot, add the pumpkin and onion and cook for 5 minutes on each side or until soft and golden. Set aside.

5 Divide the dough into 4 portions and roll into rounds $^3/_8$ in (3 mm) thick. Place the dough rounds on the lightly oiled barbecue and cook for 3–5 minutes or until brown and crisp. Turn over, top with the pumpkin, onion, feta, thyme and black pepper and cook for 4–6 minutes longer or until the pizza crust is crisp, golden and cooked through. Serve immediately.

Serves 6   **Preparation** 1½–2 hrs   **Cooking** 20 mins
Calories 442   **Fat** 26g

pizza

deep-pan

vegetable pizza

1 tsp dried yeast

12 oz (350 g) plain flour

large pinch of salt

4 tbsp olive oil, plus extra for
brushing and oiling

Topping

9 oz (250 g) can chopped
tomatoes, drained

2 tbsp tomato paste

4 tsp olive oil

2 cloves garlic, crushed

20 fresh spinach leaves

4¹/₂ oz (125 g) button
mushrooms, thinly sliced

1 red pepper, seeded and
chopped

¹/₂ red onion, chopped

4¹/₂ oz (125 g) zucchinis, sliced

¹/₂ tsp each dried oregano
and thyme

4¹/₂ oz (125 g) grated mozzarella

1 Put the yeast and water into a bowl and stir. Leave for 5–10 minutes, until frothy. Sift the flour and salt into another bowl and make a well in the center. Mix in the yeast liquid and oil to form a dough. Knead for 5 minutes or until the dough is smooth and elastic.

2 Lightly brush a bowl with oil. Put the dough in the bowl, cover with oiled plastic food wrap and leave in a warm place for 1 hour or until it has doubled in size. Preheat the oven to 400°F.

3 Knead the dough briefly, then roll out or press to fit a 12 in (30 cm) springform pan. Mix together the tomatoes and tomato paste, then spread over the base of the pizza. Heat 2 teaspoons of the oil in a saucepan, add the garlic and spinach and cook, stirring, for 3 minutes or until the spinach wilts. Drain and arrange over the tomatoes.

4 Top the pizza with the remaining vegetables, herbs and mozzarella. Drizzle the rest of the oil over and cook for 30 minutes or until golden.

***Serves** 4   **Preparation** 1–1¹/₂ hrs*
***Cooking** 33 mins   **Calories** 657   **Fat** 31g*

meat
and seafood pizza

13 oz (375 g) puff pastry, thawed if frozen

2 onions

½ oz (15 g) butter

8 slices Parma ham (Prosciutto)

2 oz (60 g) Parmesan cheese, freshly grated

pepper

chopped chives

onion
and ham pizza

1 Roll out the pastry on a floured surface, as thinly as possible. Cut out circles 3 in (7½ cm) in diameter [or 3 in (7½ cm) squares]. Put the pastry circles onto a baking tray, prick very well all over with a fork, and chill for 20 minutes.

2 Fry the onions in the butter until soft and golden. Drain on absorbent kitchen paper. Trim the Parma ham, and cut into ribbon strips.

3 Cover the pastry circles with the cooked onion, scatter the Parma ham strips around, then the cheese, pepper and some chives. Bake in a 450°F oven until crisp and golden (about 15 minutes).

Serves 4–6 **Preparation** 30 mins **Cooking** 15 mins
Calories 337 **Fat** 21g

polenta

pizza

10 oz (300 g) lean pork mince

2 tbsp chopped fresh basil

$1/2$ tsp black pepper

2 cloves garlic, crushed

$1/4$ cup chopped spring onions

$6^1/_2$ oz (185 g) polenta

2 oz (60 g) self-raising flour

1 tsp baking powder

$5^1/_2$ oz (150 mL) milk

3 tbsp tomato paste

1 cup grated mozzarella cheese

1 red pepper, seeded and cut into thin slices

$1/2$ cup olives

2 tbsp chopped fresh parsley

Serves 4-6
Preparation 15 mins
Cooking 45 mins
Calories 45 mins
Fat 10 g

1 Combine the pork with the basil, pepper, garlic and spring onions; mix well and set aside.

2 To make the pizza base, combine the polenta, flour and baking powder in a large bowl, make a well, pour in the milk and gradually mix together to form a sticky dough. Turn the dough onto a lightly floured surface and knead it for 3 minutes. Press into a greased, 10 in (25 cm) pizza tray, pinching up the edges to form a rim.

3 Spread the tomato paste over the top, sprinkle half the cheese over and decoratively arrange the pepper strips in a wheel shape on top. Arrange the olives and sprinkle with the remaining cheese and parsley. Bake in a 360°F oven for 45 minutes.

meat-lover's

pizza

9 oz (250 g) very lean ground beef

sprinkle of seasoned pepper

salt, to taste

2 tbsp tomato salsa dip (medium-hot)

shredded light cheese

sprinkle of chopped chives

fresh parsley, chopped

sprinkle of ground paprika

Serves 2
Preparation 5 mins
Cooking 10 mins
Calories 87
Fat 3g

1 Heat an electric frying pan on high until hot. Line with baking paper. Press the ground beef onto the baking paper to form base of the pizza. Sprinkle with seasoned pepper and salt. Cook, covered, on high until the ground beef changes color. Turn the meat and continue to cook for a few minutes.

2 Place the salsa, cheese, chopped chives, parsley and paprika on the ground beef, cover and cook on medium, for 5–7 minutes or until the cheese melts. Serve with vegetables as a main meal or with salad as a snack with crusty bread.

anchovy
pizza

4 tbsp olive oil	1 egg
5 onions, cut in half and thinly sliced	1/2 cup milk
	2 oz (60 g) anchovy filets in oil, drained
2 cloves garlic, chopped	
1 tsp chopped thyme	1–2 tsp tomato paste
1 tbsp chopped rosemary	18 black olives, pitted and cut in half
salt and pepper	
2 cups self-rising flour	

1 Heat 3 tablespoons of the oil in a frying pan and add the onions, garlic and herbs. Cover and cook over a moderately low heat for 10–15 minutes, stirring regularly, until the onions are soft and a light golden color. Season with salt and pepper and leave to cool.

2 Sift the flour into a bowl and mix in the egg and milk to make a firm dough. Place the dough on a floured surface and knead until smooth. Roll out into an oblong shape measuring 12 x 10 in (30 x 25 cm). Place on an oiled baking sheet.

3 Soak the anchovies in water for 5 minutes, drain on paper towels, then cut in half lengthwise. Cover the dough with the tomato paste to within 1 in (2 1/2 cm) of the rim, and spread the onion mixture over the paste. Arrange the anchovies in a lattice pattern on top and place the olive halves in each section. Drizzle the remaining oil over. Place in a preheated oven at 400°F and bake for 12–15 minutes or until the crust is golden brown.

Serves 6   **Preparation** 20 mins   **Cooking** 20–30 mins
Calories 351   **Fat** 15g

Whole-wheat pizza dough

3 tsp sugar

$^1/_4$ oz (7 g) active dry yeast

I cup warm water

2 cups whole-wheat flour

I $^1/_4$ cups plain flour

$^1/_4$ cup vegetable oil

Topping

2 tbsp tomato paste

I cup bottled tomato pasta sauce

14 oz (400 g) canned pineapple pieces in natural juices, drained

4 oz (125 g) lean ham, chopped

I red pepper, sliced

4 spring onions, chopped

2 oz (60 g) reduced-fat grated mozzarella cheese

2 tbsp chopped fresh parsley

1 To make the dough, place the sugar, yeast and $^1/_4$ cup water in a bowl and whisk with a fork until the yeast dissolves. Set aside in a warm draft-free place for 5 minutes or until the mixture is foamy.

2 Sift the whole-wheat flour and plain flour together into a bowl. Return the husks to bowl. Stir in the oil, yeast mixture and remaining water and mix to make a soft dough. Turn onto a lightly floured surface and knead for 10 minutes or until the dough is smooth and glossy.

3 Place the dough in a lightly oiled bowl, cover with plastic food wrap and set aside in a warm draft-free place for 1 hour or until doubled in volume. Punch the dough down and divide into 2 equal portions.

4 Preheat the oven to 430°F. On a lightly floured surface roll out the dough to form two 12 in (30 cm) rounds. Place the pizza bases on lightly greased baking trays and spread with tomato paste. Spread with the pasta sauce and top with the pineapple pieces, ham and red pepper. Sprinkle with then spring onions, cheese and parsley and bake for 20 minutes or until the bases are crisp and cooked.

herbed
ham and pineapple pizza

Serves 8   **Preparation** 1½ hrs   **Cooking** 20 mins
Calories 276   **Fat** 10g

salami,

ham and pineapple

Base

10$\frac{1}{2}$ oz (350 g) strong plain flour

$\frac{1}{3}$ tsp salt

1$\frac{1}{2}$ tsp dried yeast

pinch of superfine sugar

2 tbsp olive oil, plus extra for greasing

Topping

14 oz (400 g) can chopped tomatoes with herbs

3$\frac{1}{2}$ oz (100 g) peppered salami or pepperoni, cut into strips

10 oz (285 g) jar seasoned artichokes, drained

8 oz (250 g) baby plum tomatoes, halved lengthways

3$\frac{1}{2}$ oz (100 g) mozzarella, diced

1$\frac{1}{2}$ oz (40 g) pitted black olives

1 Preheat the oven to 430°F. For the topping, place the canned tomatoes in a saucepan. Simmer, uncovered, for 10–15 minutes, stirring occasionally, until reduced to a thick paste. Set aside while you make the base.

2 Mix the flour, salt, yeast and sugar in a large bowl. Make a well in the center. Mix the oil with 7 oz (200 mL) of tepid water, then gradually pour into the well, drawing the flour from the edges to make a dough and adding more water if needed.

3 Turn out the dough onto a lightly floured surface and knead for 10 minutes or until smooth and elastic. Roll out to a 12 in (30 cm) round and place on a greased baking sheet, pressing with your knuckles to make a slightly raised edge. Spread the cooked tomatoes over the pizza base and top with the salami or pepperoni, artichokes, plum tomatoes, mozzarella and olives. Cook for 20–25 minutes, until golden.

Serves *4* **Preparation** *30 mins* **Cooking** *30–40 mins*
Calories *630* **Fat** *26g*

pizza

oriental chicken pizza

1 packaged 12 in (30 cm) pizza base, or 1 serving pizza dough (see page 5)

¹/₄ cup thick teriyaki sauce

2 boneless chicken breast filets, cooked and sliced

4 oz (125 g) snow peas, thinly sliced

4 spring onions, sliced

5¹/₂ oz (155 g) tofu, chopped

6 asparagus spears, cut into 2 in (5 cm) pieces

3 tbsp chopped fresh coriander

3 tbsp sesame seeds, toasted

2 tbsp sweet chilli sauce

Serves *4* ***Preparation*** *20 mins*
Cooking *30 mins*
Calories *762* ***Fat*** *35g*

1 Place the pizza base on a lightly greased baking tray. Spread the base with the teriyaki sauce and top with the chicken, snow peas, spring onions, tofu and asparagus. Sprinkle with coriander and sesame seeds.

2 Drizzle the chilli sauce over the pizza and bake in a preheated 430°F oven for 30 minutes or until base is golden and crisp.

pizzas
from the bread
making machine

herbed *pizza base*

½ cup tepid water

1 tbsp olive oil or canola oil

½ tsp salt

½ tsp sugar

½ clove garlic, crushed

½ tsp dried oregano

2 tbsp chopped fresh parsley

2 cups white flour

1 tsp dry yeast

Serves 4
Preparation 1½ hrs–2 hrs
Cooking 5–10 mins
Calories 293
Fat 5g

1 Place all the ingredients into the bread pan in the order listed, insert into the bread maker and close the lid. Program: Pizza Dough or Dough. Press: Start

2 Divide the completed dough into three. Roll each into a circle approximately 5½ in (14 cm) in diameter. Place onto greased baking trays, cover and stand for 10 minutes to rise.

3 Brush with olive oil and sprinkle with red chilli and garlic. Bake in a preheated oven at 480°F for 5–10 minutes.

4 When cooked, place on plate and top with salad greens and marinated roasted vegetables such as eggplant, semi-dried tomatoes and zucchini.

tomato and olive pizza

Dough

5 oz (150 mL) tepid water

1 tbsp olive oil

½ tsp salt

1 tsp sugar

1 cup white flour

1 tsp dry yeast

Topping

7 oz (200 mL) pizza sauce

3 tomatoes, sliced

1¾ oz (50 g) black olives

capers, to taste

fresh herbs of choice, such as basil or thyme

Serves 4 **Preparation** 2 hrs
Cooking 20–25 mins
Calories 232 **Fat** 6g

1 Place all the ingredients into the bread pan in the order listed, insert into the bread maker and close the lid.

2 Preheat the oven to 380°F. Turn the completed dough onto a lightly floured surface. Knead into a ball and roll into a circle. With oiled fingers press into an oiled 10 in (25 cm) pizza tray. Cover with a dish towel; stand in a warm place to rise for 20 minutes. Brush with oil and spread with the pizza sauce. Arrange the remaining topping ingredients in the order given over the surface. Bake for 20–25 minutes or until cooked.

calzone loaf

Bread dough

I cup tepid water	I clove garlic, crushed
1/4 cup olive oil	I red pepper, seeded and chopped
I tsp sugar	
1/4 tsp salt	I medium eggplant, diced
14 oz (400 g) white flour	8 oz (250 g) feta cheese, diced
1 1/2 tsp dry yeast	3 oz (100 g) grated Parmesan cheese

Filling

3 tbsp olive oil	I tbsp chopped fresh parsley
I medium red onion, chopped	I tsp dried thyme or sage
	salt and pepper, to taste
	egg and water for brushing
	I tbsp toasted sesame seeds

1 Place the ingredients into the bread pan in the order listed, insert into the bread maker and close the lid. Program: Dough. Press: Start Meanwhile prepare the filling.

2 Heat the olive oil in a saucepan; add the onion, garlic, pepper and eggplant. Stir fry a little then place the lid on the saucepan and allow to simmer for 10 minutes, stirring occasionally. Remove from the heat and allow to cool. Add the cheeses, parsley and seasonings.

3 Turn the completed dough onto a lightly floured surface, punch down then roll out to a rectangle, 10 x 15 in (25 x 38 cm).

Serves *4*   ***Preparation*** *2 hrs*   ***Cooking*** *40 mins*
Calories *830*   ***Fat*** *46g*

4 With the longer side in front of you (parallel to the bench edge) spread the filling across the center in a 3 in (7 cm) wide strip and 1 in (2 cm) in from each end. Wet the edges of the dough with egg glaze. Lift both sides of the dough over the filling to meet edge to edge in the center. Rope fold or flute the seam to seal and tuck the ends underneath. Place on a greased baking tray, cover and stand in a warm place to rise for 20 minutes.

5 Brush well with the egg wash and sprinkle with sesame seeds. Bake in a pre-heated oven at 400°F for 30 minutes or until golden and cooked.

weights and measures

quick converter

(cook's conversions are not exact)

Metric	Imperial
5mm	$1/4$in
1cm	$1/2$in
2cm	$3/4$in
$2^{1}/_{2}$cm	1in
5cm	2in
$10^{1}/_{2}$cm	4in
15cm	6in
20cm	8in
23cm	9in
25cm	10in
30cm	12in

metric cups and spoons

(cook's conversions are not exact)

Metric	Cups	Imperial
63mL	$1/4$ cup	$2^{1}/_{4}$fl oz
85mL	$1/3$ cup	3 floz
125mL	$1/2$ cup	$4^{1}/_{2}$fl oz
250mL	1 cup	$8^{3}/_{4}$fl oz
Metric	**Spoons**	
$1^{1}/_{4}$mL	$1/4$ teaspoon	
$2^{1}/_{2}$mL	$1/2$ teaspoon	
5mL	1 teaspoon	
20mL	1 tablespoon	

measuring liquids

(cook's conversions are not exact)

Metric	Imperial	
30mL	1fl oz	
55mL	2fl oz	
85mL	3fl oz	
115mL	4fl oz	
125mL	$4^{1}/_{2}$fl oz	($1/2$ cup)
150mL	$5^{1}/_{4}$fl oz	
170mL	6fl oz	
185mL	$6^{1}/_{2}$fl oz	
200mL	7fl oz	
225mL	8fl oz	
250mL	$8^{3}/_{4}$fl oz	(1 cup)
285mL	10fl oz	
370mL	13fl oz	
400mL	14fl oz	
500mL	$17^{1}/_{2}$fl oz	(2 cups)
570mL	20fl oz	(1 pint)
1 litre	$35^{1}/_{3}$fl oz	(4 cups)

oven temperatures

°C	°F	Gas Mark
120	250	$1/4$
140	275	1
150	300	2
160	325	3
180	350	4
190	375	5
200	400	6
220	425	7
240	475	8
250	500	9

measuring dry ingredients

(cook's conversions are not exact)

Metric	Imperial
15g	$^1/_2$oz
20g	$^2/_3$oz
30g	1oz
55g	2oz
85g	3oz
115g	4oz ($^1/_4$lb)
125g	4$^1/_2$oz
140g	5oz
170g	6oz
200g	7oz
225g	8oz ($^1/_2$lb)
255g	9oz
315g	11oz
370g	13oz
400g	14oz
425g	15oz
455g	16oz (1 lb)
500g	17$^1/_2$oz
680g	1$^1/_2$lb
1kg	2lb 3oz
1$^1/_2$kg	3lb 5oz

Disclaimer: The nutritional information listed under each recipe does not include the nutrient content of garnishes or any accompaniments not listed in specific quantities in the ingredient list. The nutritional information for each recipe is an estimate only, and may vary depending on the brand of ingredients used, and the natural biological variations in the composition of natural foods such as meat, fish, fruit and vegetables. The nutritional information was calculated by using Foodworks dietary analysis software (Version 3, Xyris Software Pty Ltd, Highgate Hill, Queensland, Australia) based on the Australian food composition tables and food manufacturers' data. Where not specified, ingredients are always analyzed as average or medium; not small or large.

index